Bakemoji !

Bakemoji !

Emoji Cupcakes, Cakes, and Baking
Sure To Put a Smile on Any Occasion

Written by: **Marion Beilin**
Photography by: **Amandine Honegger**
Design by: **Sylvie Rost**

Skyhorse Publishing

Introduction

Emojis, or "emoticons," are happy little pictures that have totally become part of our everyday lives. Yet, weren't their forefathers the "XOXOs" from our parents? Simple circle-with-a-smile emojis have evolved into multi-colored figures enriched by expressions and social attributes. And they keep on changing, offering even more ways to express yourself . . . without having to write a thing!

Now found in places well beyond the cell phones always at our disposal, it's only natural that emojis also make their way into cuisine. All you'll need to start transforming crêpes, cookies, cakes, and more into emojis is some fruit sauce, chocolate, and candy. Afterwards come the cookie cutters, stencils, trimming, sugar paste icing, and food decorating pens, turning a simple sponge cake into a gourmet party hat or heart.

Use—or overuse—the premade decorations and adornments found in most supermarkets, but don't hesitate to open your cupboards and fridge: blueberries, cherry tomatoes, and carrot slices all make great eyes. Cream cheese with a little sugar and vanilla? That's all you need to make a quick icing.

Above all, don't hesitate to alter the recipes to suit your tastes and the messages that you want to get across. You'll find nothing says it better than your emoji cakes!

—Marion Beilin

About Me

As a former food and travel journalist, I have traveled all around the world for different magazines. At the same time, I decided to get my CAP Pastry Diploma as an independent candidate. Nowadays, I advise hotels, restaurants, chefs, and independent pastry chefs. I have written several cookbooks, too, including *Le quinoa et autres graines pleines d'énergie*, in the "J'Adore" collection.

Table of Contents

The Golden Recipe

Unicorn Shortbreads from Roxane's Workshop **9**

Emoji Baking: Starting Out **10**

Supplies Section **12**

Key Tips **13**

Step-by-Step Recipe Lesson: Homemade Sugar Paste **14**

Cookies and Tarts **16**

Iced Emoji Sugar Cookies **18**

Feet Cookies **20**

Cloud Shortbreads **22**

Chocolate Side Eye Cookies **24**

Cake Pops **26**

Pig Biscuits **30**

Poop Cupcakes **32**

French Ice Cream Macarons **34**

Poop Meringues **36**

Cakes **38**

Apple of My Eye Cake **40**

Gift Cake **42**

Party Hat **46**

Christmas Tree **48**

Banzai Marble Cake **50**

Snowman **52**

"Hello There!" Cake **54**

Cheesecake Heart **56**

Ghost Cake (lactose-free!) **58**

Broken Heart Cake **60**

Pancakes, Waffles, Mousses, etc. **62**

Waffles **64**

Mini Love Pancakes **68**

"Hurts So Good" Chocolate Mousse **70**

Rice Pudding **72**

Angry Panna Cotta **74**

Savory Recipes **76**

Kissing Omelet **78**

Mini Pizzas **80**

Stunned Zucchini Tart **82**

Potato, Bacon, and Cheddar Quiche **84**

Mini Thumbs Up Grilled Ham and Cheese Sandwiches **88**

Semolina Tartlets **90**

Small Bites + Gourmet Selection **92**

Useful Measurements **94**

Index **95**

Unicorn Shortbreads

MAKES ABOUT 25 COOKIES

Preparation Time: 20 minutes

Bake Time: 11 minutes

For the cookies:

2 cups of flour

1 cup of powdered sugar

1 packet of vanilla sugar

1 pinch of salt

½ cup of butter

1 egg

For the icing:

1 egg white

2 ⅔ cups of powdered sugar

1 tsp. of lemon juice

Various food colorings

Prepare the cookies. Preheat the oven to 350°F. Mix the flour, powdered sugar, vanilla sugar, and salt in a bowl. Cut the cold butter into small pieces, add these in, and then work the ingredients together with your fingertips until you have a fine powder. Incorporate the egg and mix to obtain a smooth dough. Shape the dough into a ball, wrap it in plastic, and set aside in the refrigerator for 1 hour. Roll out the dough, then use a unicorn cookie cutter or a unicorn stencil that you cut out from cardboard to form the cookies.

Place the cookies on an oven tray covered in baking paper and bake for 11 minutes.

Prepare the icing. Using an electric beater, mix together the egg white, powdered sugar, and lemon juice. Divide the icing into several bowls and add the different food colorings. Make sure to leave 1 white.

Fill each of your piping bags with a different color of icing and make a little hole at one end. Use a dark purple to trace the cookie's outline, then draw the mane and the muzzle. Let the cookies air dry for 20 minutes.

Fill in the open spaces with the different colored icings. If necessary, add some drops of water or lemon juice to the icing for a more liquid consistency.

About Me

My name is Roxane, and I'm the mother of 2 little pipsqueaks. Just 3 years ago, I developed a taste for pastries. Now I find myself thrown into the crazy adventures of YouTube through my channel, Roxane's Workshop, where I present easy family-friendly recipes. To me, "pastry making" is a synonym of "sharing."

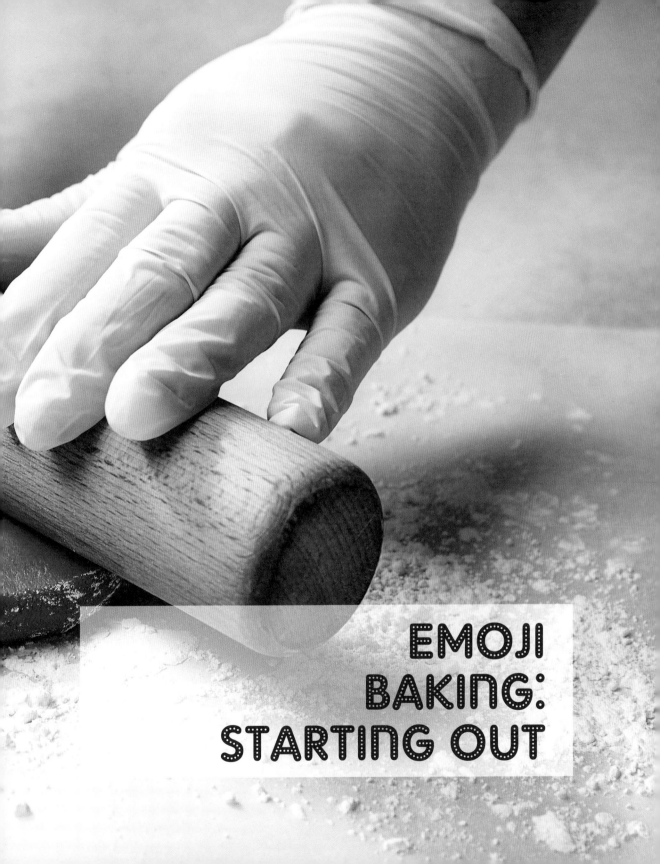

EMOJI BAKING: STARTING OUT

Supplies section

Basic Utensils:
- Mixing bowl
- Bowl
- Spatula
- Electric beater
- Food processor
- Whisk
- Piping bag(s) and several nozzles of different sizes
- Sharp kitchen knives
- Vegetable peeler
- Rubber spatula
- Rolling pin
- Cookie cutter
- Kitchen scale
- Measuring cups
- Colander/sieve
- Scissors
- Parchment paper
- Pie dish/cake pan
- Springform pan with a removable bottom
- Muffin/cupcake tin
- Ramekins
- Toothpicks
- Measuring spoons
- Popsicle sticks

Also:
- Food decorating pens
- Chocolate spread
- Small edible cake decorations shaped like hearts, eyes, stars, etc.
- Candies
- Almond paste or sugar paste

Key Tips:

First, keep in mind that the purpose of this book is to have fun (and, of course, to enjoy these delicious, fun recipes)! Feel free to experiment by adding a little more flour, a bit less sugar, green food coloring instead of yellow, swapping fruits for bonbons . . . use your imagination!

Before starting a recipe, take out all the ingredients and check that you're not missing any. It would be a shame to begin making a cake and then realize that you've run out of sugar or baking powder.

"Let your imagination run wild!"

Feel free to **use a food processor or an electric beater**. This will make tasks easier, and sometimes it will even be necessary in order to whip egg whites into stiff peaks. It will also help you save time. Consider rinsing off the utensils right after using them, as it is much easier to clean them then.

Don't invest right away in all the materials used by professional pastry artists. Open your cupboards and you'll find cups or glasses that can serve as cookie-cutters, small knives to cut out shapes from sugar paste . . . even when using baking pans with a bland, classic shape, you can still cut the cake in the size and shape you want for a nice final product!

In the pastry arts, **larger surfaces beg for more accessories and decorations**. Imagine what you could make with multi-colored sprinkles, gold and silver nonpareils, white stars . . . and don't worry if you don't use these when making a particular recipe, they keep for a very long time, so you'll have plenty of chances to use them. Have fun!

Browsing online is good for finding recipe ideas and tutorials, ordering utensils/supplies, food coloring, molds/tins, decorations, etc. It's a goldmine!

Step-by-Step Recipe Lesson: Homemade Sugar Paste

FOR A LARGE CAKE, ABOUT 10 INCHES
(And you'll still have paste left over)
Preparation Time: 15 minutes

1 egg white

Food coloring

2 tbsps. of liquid honey

3 cups of powdered sugar + a little for the countertop and the rolling pin

Notes

☺ If you don't use the paste right away, wrap it tightly in kitchen wrap and store it in a cupboard, rather than in the refrigerator or freezer, as it won't keep well with the moisture, and the cold will harden it. Wrapped and in a cupboard, you can store it for a few weeks.

☺ If possible, make your decorations from the sugar paste just before serving your cake or cookies, as the paste tends to dry out quite quickly.

☺ It's not necessary to have a special rolling pin for sugar paste, but you will need a lot of powdered sugar to keep the paste from sticking to your everyday rolling pin. So if you become a fan of pastry arts . . . invest in one!

In a large mixing bowl, mix together the egg white, the food coloring of your choice, and the honey, then gradually add the powdered sugar while stirring throughout. *(step 1 and 2)*

As it begins to thicken, shape it with your fingers. Add the powdered sugar until the paste is no longer sticky. Consider wearing thin gloves to protect your hands from food coloring stains. *(step 3)*

When the paste is supple and not tacky, spread it on the countertop using a rolling pin. Remember to first sprinkle a little powdered sugar on the countertop and rolling pin so that the paste won't stick too much. *(step 4)*

TARTS & COOKIES

Iced Emoji Sugar Cookies

MAKES ABOUT 35 COOKIES

Preparation Time: 20 minutes

Baking Time: 10 minutes

Refrigerate: 30 minutes

Let sit before serving: 1 hour
and 30 minutes

½ cup of butter

*1⅕ cups of flour + a little to
spread*

1 cup of fine powdered sugar

*Slightly under ¼ cup (1¼ oz.)
ground almonds*

1 egg (beaten)

For the royal icing:

1 egg white

2 tsps. of lemon juice

2⅔ cups of powdered sugar

Various food colorings

Cut the butter into little pieces. Mix the sugar, flour, and ground almonds in a bowl. Add the butter and knead using your fingertips. When the mixture gets a grainy consistency, incorporate the already-beaten egg. Stir until the batter is even. Shape into a ball, then flatten a bit. Wrap in plastic and refrigerate for at least 30 minutes.

Preheat the oven to 350°F. With a pastry rolling pin covered in flour, spread the dough until it is ⅛ inch thick. Using a cookie cutter or a glass, cut out small circles and place the cookies on a baking sheet covered in parchment paper. Bake for 10 minutes, then take the cookies out and let them cool.

Prepare the royal icing. Mix the egg white and lemon juice. Pour in the powdered sugar little by little while stirring. Add a few drops of water if the mixture is too thick. The icing should not be too runny, as you'll need it later to decorate the edges of the cookies.

Divide the icing into 2 parts: ⅓ and ⅔. Add some yellow food coloring to ⅔ of the icing. Split the remaining ⅓ in 2 or 3 parts, depending on how many colors you want, and add a few drops of your chosen food dye to each. Mix well. Pour some yellow icing into a piping bag with a fine/writing nozzle. Trace the cookies' outlines. Let them dry for 30 minutes. Dilute the remaining yellow icing with a few drops of water, then use it to fill inside the lines you drew before. Let the cookies dry for about 1 hour.

Pour the other icing colors into different piping bags with nozzles. Delicately draw on the cookies the shapes you want in your chosen colors. For example: black for eyes, mouths and eyebrows; blue for tears, water drops, ZZZs; white for teeth.

Feet Cookies

MAKES 6 COOKIES

Preparation Time: 20 minutes

Baking Time: 12 minutes
per batch

⅔ cup blond cane sugar

½ cup of softened butter

1 egg

1 ½ cups of flour

1 pinch of salt

⅔ cup of chocolate chips
(dark, milk, white, caramel, etc.)
+ ¼ cup for decorating

Preheat the oven to 400°F.

Put the sugar and softened butter (soft enough to dent it with a poke, but far from melted!) in a mixing bowl. Using an electric mixer, beat the mixture until creamy. Add the egg and beat again. Incorporate the flour and salt, then stir with a large spoon. Then pour in the chocolate and mix delicately.

Cover 2 baking sheets with parchment paper. Divide the dough into sixths and shape each piece into a ball. Place these evenly spaced on the baking sheets. Gently flatten the cookies.

Close your hand into a fist. Lay your fist flat into the cookie. Your thumb should press into the top of the cookie to form the big toe. Next, make 4 indents with your index finger for the other toes. Now you have a foot! Repeat for each cookie. Bake the batch for about 12 minutes.

Take the cookies out of the oven. If the cookies are not clearly shaped like feet, use a spoon or the handle of a knife to redraw the outlines and press down on the center. Let them cool on the baking sheet. Delicately remove the cookies from the baking sheets and put them onto a plate. Gently melt the chocolate chips in a double boiler or microwave and, using a brush, "paint" the feet with chocolate.

Notes

☺ Be sure to leave enough space between the cookies on the tray: The dough will spread while baking and the cookies will end up touching each other.
☺ You can finish decorating by adding some dried fruit.

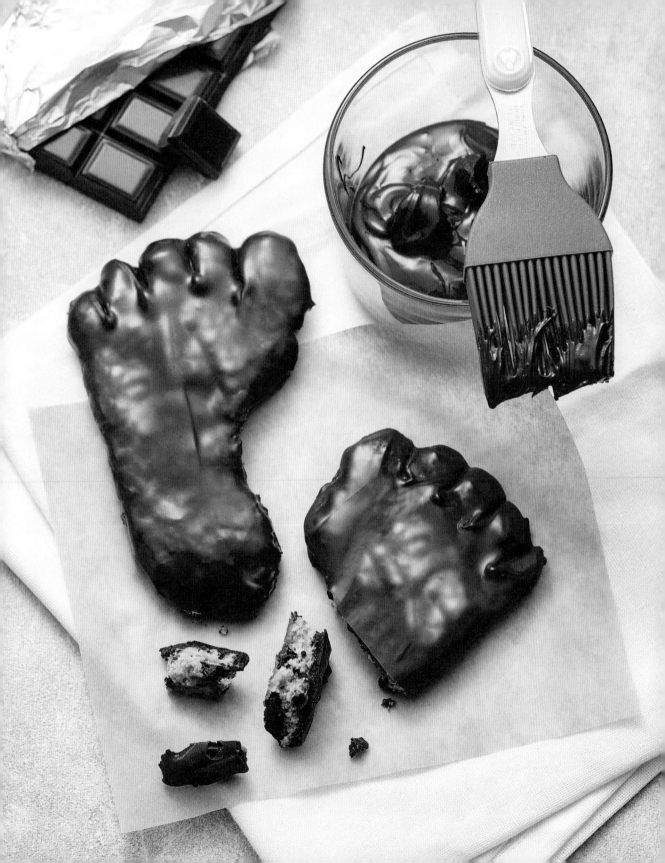

Cloud Shortbreads

½ cup of butter

1 cup of powdered sugar

1⅕ cups of flour + a little to spread

Slightly under ½ cup of ground almonds

1 egg (beaten)

For the royal icing:

1 egg white

2 tsps. of lemon juice

2 ⅓ cups of powdered sugar

To decorate:

2 oz. of Good & Plenty

Cut the butter into small pieces. In a bowl, mix together the sugar, flour, and ground almonds. Add the butter and knead with your fingers. When the dough becomes grainy, add the already-beaten egg. Stir until the batter is even. Then shape the dough into a ball and slightly flatten it. Wrap in plastic and place in the refrigerator for at least 30 minutes.

Preheat the oven to 350°F. Using a pastry rolling pin covered in flour, roll out the dough until it is about ⅛ inch thick. With a cookie cutter, cut out small shortbreads shaped like clouds and place these on a baking sheet covered in greaseproof paper. Bake for 10 minutes, then remove the batch from the oven and let it cool.

Prepare the royal icing. Mix the egg white and lemon juice. Gradually pour in the powdered sugar while mixing. If the mixture is too thick, add a few drops of water. However, the icing shouldn't be too runny, as you'll need it later to decorate the shortbreads' edges.

Pour the icing into a piping bag with a fine nozzle. Trace the outlines of the cookies. Let dry for 30 minutes. Dilute the icing and fill in between the outlines. Allow about 1 hour to dry.

Put the cloud shortbreads onto a plate (you could also put them on a cake, a crepe, a waffle, a slice of brioche!), then arrange the Good & Plenty like raindrops.

Notes

☺ You can make stencils by drawing clouds of various sizes on paper and then cutting them out.

☺ Place these stencils onto the dough and cut along the outlines using the tip of a very sharp knife.

☺ Add a little cinnamon or citrus zest (organic or untreated, that's key!)

Chocolate
Side Eye Cookies

MAKES ABOUT 15 EYES

Preparation Time: 20 minutes

Baking Time: 20 minutes

Refrigerate: 1 hour

2 cups of flour + a little for the countertop

⁴/₅ cup of unsweetened cocoa powder

½ tsp. of baking soda

1 cup softened butter at room temperature

¾ cup brown sugar

1 pinch of salt

For the vanilla cream:

1 ⅔ cups of powdered sugar

½ cup of softened butter at room temperature

2 packets of vanilla sugar

Prepare the cookies. Sift together the flour, cocoa powder, and baking soda.

Use a food processor or electric mixer to soften the butter. Add the brown sugar and beat until creamy. With a spatula, move the butter to the center of the bowl. Add half of the flour-cocoa mixture. Stir, then add the other half. Continue stirring until the batter is even, then roll it into a ball. Flatten it a little, then wrap completely in plastic and let chill for at least 1 hour.

Preheat the oven to 325°F. Spread a piece of parchment paper onto a baking tray. Sprinkle flour on the counter.

Roll out the dough with a pastry rolling pin. Use an oval cookie cutter to make the eyes, then use a smaller, round cookie cutter for the irises. If you don't have cookie cutters, make an oval and a circle from a piece of paper. Place these stencils onto the dough and cut around them with a sharp knife. Gather the leftover dough together and repeat these steps.

Bake for about 15 minutes, until the cookies just begin to crack along the surface. Remove from the oven and let them cool down.

Prepare the cream. Soften the butter with a whisk. Add the powdered sugar and vanilla sugar. Whisk gently for 1 minute, then raise your speed and continue whisking for another minute until you have a thick cream. Pour this into a piping bag. Spread the cream over 2 oval cookies. Place 2 small round cookies on the sides of the oval cookies, for the side eye effect. Repeat these steps with the rest of the cookies and cream. Finish by putting a small dot of vanilla cream on the round cookies.

Cake Pops

MAKES 10 POPS

Preparation Time: 30 minutes

Baking Time: 5 to 10 minutes

Let sit before serving: 10 minutes

10 sandwich cookies with vanilla cream, e.g., Oreo (or use the eye recipe on p. 24)

7 oz. of yellow Candy Melts or white chocolate chips + yellow food coloring

10 Popsicle sticks

Red and black food decorating pens

Notes

☺ Candy Melts are easy to find online.

☺ Very sugary, these little pastilles are perfect and very practical.

☺ Add hearts, tears, stars, etc. made from sugar paste (recipe on p. 14) or almond paste
(recipe on p. 92)—all decorations which you can stick on with a little chocolate.

Gently separate the Oreo cookies in 2 and place both halves on parchment paper. Put a mixing bowl on top of a pan of simmering water, add the Candy Melts or chocolate, and gently melt in the double boiler. If you opt instead for the microwave, use low power and stir often. If you use chocolate, add a little food coloring and stir.

Place a popsicle stick in the middle of each cream-side cookie. Then dab 1 ½ teaspoons of melted Candy Melts or chocolate onto the middle. Close the cookie by putting the plain half on top. Press down lightly and let it rest for 10 minutes.

If the remaining melted Candy Melts or chocolate have hardened, reheat it. When the mixture is soft again, dunk each pop into the melt. Let the excess drip off a little, then place each pop flat on the parchment paper. Let the coating cool completely and harden. Once it is quite cool, draw emoticon expressions on the pops with the food decorating pens.

Pig Biscuits

MAKES ABOUT 20 COOKIES

Preparation Time: 20 minutes

Baking Time: 10 minutes

Refrigerate: 30 minutes

Let sit before serving: 1 hour
and 30 minutes

½ cup of butter

1 cup of fine powdered sugar

1 ⅕ cups of flour + a bit
to spread

Slightly under ½ cup of
ground almonds

1 egg

Some drops of red
food coloring

3 tbsps. of red (strawberry,
raspberry, redcurrant, etc.) jam

Black food decorating pen

About forty raisins or chocolate
chips or other little candies

Cut the butter into small pieces. In a bowl, mix the sugar, flour, and ground almonds. Add the butter and mix using your fingers until the consistency becomes grainy. Beat the egg with some food coloring and add this to the dough. Stir well until the batter is even.

Separate the dough into 2 different-sized pieces (⅓ and ⅔, respectively). Make 2 balls, flatten these a bit, wrap in plastic and place in the refrigerator for a minimum of 30 minutes.

Preheat the oven to 350°F.

With a pastry rolling pin covered in flour, roll out the larger ball of dough until it is about ⅛ inch thick. Using a round cookie cutter, cut out 20 sugar cookies (the pigs' heads). Place these onto a baking sheet covered with parchment paper. Gather the rest of the dough, form another ball, then tear off some small pieces to make the ears. Roll these between your palms, flatten them, lightly wet one side, and stick the ears to the sides of the round cookies.

Roll out the other ball of dough. Cut out some smaller circles for the snouts. Place the snouts onto the tray with the other cookies and bake for 10 minutes (watch closely that these do not brown too much). Remove from the oven and let them cool down. At the center of each pig's head, put a little jam, then stick the snout there by pressing down lightly. Draw the nostrils with the food decorating pen. Place 2 little dots of jam where the eyes would be and then stick the raisins, chocolate, or candies there.

Notes

☺ You can also draw the eyes with a food decorating pen or buy small, edible decorations in the shape of eyes.

☺ Take care not to make the ears too thin, as they will bake more quickly and then become too dark.

Poop Cupcakes

MAKES ABOUT 20
CUPCAKES

Preparation Time: 30 minutes

Cooking Time: 30 minutes

Let sit before serving:
10 minutes

For the mousse:

1 cup of dark or milk
chocolate chips

Just over ¼ stick of very soft
(but not melted!) butter

½ cup of powdered sugar

1 tbsp. of liquid honey

4½ ounces of mascarpone

For the cupcakes:

1 heaping cup of dark
chocolate chips

½ cup of very soft butter

1¼ cups of powdered sugar

3 eggs

Slightly under ⅔ cup of flour

2 tsps. of baking powder

Slightly over ¼ cup of
heavy cream

1 pinch of salt

Some leftover strips of white
sugar paste

Food decorating pen

Prepare the mousse. Mix the chocolate in a double boiler or microwave (on medium, while mixing regularly), until it is quite smooth. Let it cool.

With an electric beater, beat the soft butter to loosen it. Add the sugar and honey and beat until creamy. Pour in the melted chocolate and mix well. Incorporate the mascarpone and then mix again to create an even-textured cream. Cover and keep cool.

Preheat the oven to 350°F.

Prepare the cupcakes. Fill the cupcake molds with oven-safe cupcake liners. Melt the chocolate in a double boiler or microwave. With an electric beater, beat the butter and sugar. Add the eggs, one by one, then the flour, baking powder, salt, melted chocolate, and heavy cream. Mix until the batter is even.

Fill the molds ¾ of the way with the batter. Bake for about 20 minutes. Remove from the oven. Let rest 10 minutes before removing the cupcakes from the pan and putting them on a cooling rack.

Fill a piping bag with the mousse, then cover the tops of the cupcakes. Form mouths and eyes from the sugar paste, draw the pupils with the food decorating pen, and place these on the mousse.

Notes

☺ To change the taste or save time, feel free to replace the mousse with a simple chocolate chantilly or ganache.

☺ You can prepare the cupcakes ahead of time and even freeze them (without the mousse).

French Ice Cream Macarons

MAKES 12 MACARONS

Preparation Time: 15 minutes

Refrigerate: 10 minutes

12 small lemon or vanilla macarons

2 heaping cups of lemon (or raspberry) ice cream

1 tbsp. of marmalade made from red fruits or lemon curd

A food decorating pen

Some blueberries, strawberries, or redcurrants

Buy the macarons from a pastry shop. With a food decorating pen, delicately draw eyes and mouths with different expressions on the macarons.

Take the ice cream from the freezer. Let it soften for a few minutes. During this time, delicately separate the 2 shells of each macaron.

Using an ice cream scoop, form 12 little balls, flatten them lightly with a spatula or the back of a tablespoon. Place these in the middle of the macarons' undecorated halves, then close the macarons by putting the shells with the drawings back on top.

Place in the refrigerator for at least 10 minutes.

Just before serving, finish decorating by placing a small dollop of marmalade where each eye would be and stick a blueberry, a strawberry or a redcurrant onto it.

Notes

☺ You can choose small or large macarons, whichever you prefer. If you choose large ones, it's better to use raspberries for the eyes.

☺ Feel free to use different ice cream and macaron flavors. Serve with red fruit sauce.

Poop Meringues

MAKES 20 MERINGUES

Preparation Time: 30 minutes

Baking Time: 1 hour

2 tbsps. of unsweetened cocoa powder

½ cup of powdered sugar

½ cup granulated sugar

2 egg whites

Slightly over ⅛ cup of dark chocolate

Some mini-marshmallows

Preheat the oven to 210°F.

Sift together the cocoa powder and the powdered sugar. Using an electric mixer or a food processor, beat the egg whites until stiff while gradually raising the speed. When they begin to fluff, pour in the cocoa/powdered sugar mix little by little. Beat again for about 10 minutes, at a fast speed, until the meringue is quite firm. Add in the granulated sugar, incorporating it gently with a spatula. Pour the meringue into a piping bag with a plain nozzle.

Cover a baking sheet with parchment paper. Form little piles with the meringue, trying to make them look as much as possible like poop. Bake for 1 hour. Turn off the oven and let the meringues cool inside it.

Prepare the eyes and mouths. Cut the mini marshmallows into slices to make the eyes and into fourths for the mouths. Melt the chocolate in a double boiler or microwave (on low, stirring regularly). Then, with a toothpick, draw pupils on the non-sticky side of the marshmallow with the melted chocolate. Place the mouths and eyes onto the meringues.

Notes

☺ If the little bits of marshmallow do not seem sticky enough, add a little melted chocolate before putting them onto the meringues.

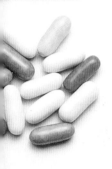

CAKES

Apple of My Eye Cake

SERVES 8 PEOPLE

Preparation Time: 25 minutes

Baking Time: 40 minutes

1⅕ cups of flour

¾ cup of sugar + a bit for the pan

½ cup of butter + a bit for the pan

4 eggs

3 apples, at least 1 red one

1 heaping tsp. of baking powder

Zest from 1 organic (or untreated) lemon

2 oz. of dark or milk chocolate

Leaves from 2 stalks of rosemary

Salt

For the cream cheese icing:

½ cup of soft (but not melted) butter

1 tsp. of vanilla

Cup of cream or soft cheese, like St Morêt or Kiri

3 cups of powdered sugar

A packet of yellow crystal sugar or coarse sanding sugar

Preheat the oven to 350°F. Melt the butter. Pluck the rosemary leaves and mince these as finely as possible. In a mixing bowl, whisk together the sugar and eggs. Add a pinch of salt, then pour in the flour and baking powder. Stir gently, then add the melted butter and rosemary. Mix well. Wash the apples with water, then dry. Cut the red apple so as to make 2 circles, with skin. Using a very sharp knife (or a cookie cutter), cut out a heart from each circle. Set aside. Peel all the apples, remove the core and seeds, then cut into small pieces. Add these to the batter along with the lemon zest, then mix using a spatula.

Butter a springform pan, sprinkle it with sugar, then pour in the batter and bake for 35 to 40 minutes.

Melt the chocolate in a double boiler or microwave. Unroll a piece of parchment paper, and delicately pour onto it a little chocolate in the shape of a mouth. Let it harden.

Prepare the icing. Place the soft butter and vanilla in a mixing bowl. Using an electric beater, mix these with the spreadable cheese or cream. Continue mixing until the texture is even. Then add the powdered sugar little by little, while still mixing.

Check the cake's doneness. Stick the tip of a knife into the center. It should come back out dry. Remove the cake from the oven, let it cool in the pan to keep it spongy. Remove from the pan by flipping it onto a plate.

Using a spatula, cover the cake in icing, smoothing it well, then add the yellow crystal sugar or coarse sanding sugar. Finish by placing the chocolate mouth on the cake along with the heart-shaped eyes.

Gift Cake

FOR 6 TO 8 PEOPLE

Preparation Time: 50 minutes

Baking Time: 30 minutes

Let sit before serving: 40 minutes

⅔ cup of butter + a bit for the pan

Slightly under 1 cup of flour + a bit for the pan

2 organic (or untreated) oranges

2 eggs

¼ packet of baking powder

Slightly under ⅔ cup of powdered sugar

10 ½ oz. of almond paste (recipe on p. 92)

¼ cup of dark chocolate

Some drops of red food coloring for the ribbon and yellow for the gift

Notes

☺ If the paste is too sticky, spread it on a piece of parchment paper
and place it for a few minutes in the freezer.

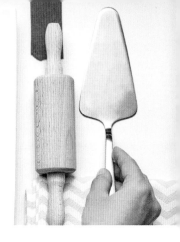

Preheat the oven to 400°F. Butter and flour a square baking pan.

Wash the oranges with water, then dry. Using a cheese grater, zest the oranges. Then press/squeeze 1 orange. Crack the eggs and beat them into a mixture. Sift together the flour and baking powder. Melt the butter in a pan over low heat. After removing from the heat, add the powdered sugar and mix until even. Add the orange juice, then the eggs. Whisk. Add the flour, baking powder, and orange zest. Stir until the batter is very smooth.

Pour the batter into the pan and bake for 10 minutes. Lower the oven temperature to 350°F and continue baking for 20 minutes. Take it out of the oven, let cool 10 minutes, remove from the pan and place on a cooling rack. With a long knife, cut the sides of the cake to shape it into a gift.

Prepare the decorations. Split the almond paste into thirds. Color the first $2/3$: spread the portion of almond paste and add the yellow food coloring. Fold the paste on itself several times so the color is even, then roll out with a rolling pin (if it's too sticky, sprinkle the rolling pin with powdered sugar or put the paste between 2 sheets of parchment paper).

The paste should be larger than the top of the cake and its sides. Place the paste on top of the cake. Press it so it sticks all the way down to the bottom, then cut away the excess with a sharp knife.

Melt the chocolate in a double boiler or microwave, pour it into a piping bag with a (fine) nozzle, then draw the lines of the gift box and its lid.

Spread the remaining almond paste and add some red food coloring. Cut 2 large strips of paste, long enough to stretch from one end of the gift to the other. Use a small spatula or a cake server to lift the strips from the countertop and place them onto the cake.

Crumple a bit of paper towel and roll it up in parchment paper to shape the ribbon. From the remaining paste, cut 2 rectangles, 6" by $1\frac{1}{2}$", then form 2 loops and slip the papers into the middle. Place each loop opposite each other at the center of the cake. Cut a small rectangle from the leftover paste and place it between the 2 loops, making sure to stick these together well. Adjust delicately by hand, to get it as close as possible to the shape of a ribbon. Chill and remove the paper just before serving.

Party Hat

SERVES 8 PEOPLE

Preparation Time: 30 minutes

Baking Time: 40 minutes

1 cup of yogurt

3 cups of flour

2 cups of sugar

3 eggs

½ cup of oil

½ packet of baking powder

1 packet of vanilla sugar

Candies for decorating

(Jelly Beans, Sour Straws, Sour Worms, etc.)

Salt

For the buttercream icing:

2 ½ cups of powdered sugar

Slightly less than a ½ cup of soft (but not melted) butter

1 tbsp. of heavy cream

Some drops of vanilla extract

Some drops of yellow food coloring

Decorations of all colors for the cake (Sprinkles, dragées/pearls, etc.)

Preheat the oven to 350°F.

Crack the eggs in a mixing bowl. Add the yogurt, stir, then pour in the sugars and a pinch of salt. Whisk vigorously. Add the flour and baking powder, then mix. Pour in the oil and mix gently at first, then with more verve. Pour the batter into a springform pan and bake for about 35 minutes. Stick the tip of a knife into the middle of the cake, it should come back out dry. Remove the cake from the pan and let it cool down.

Prepare the icing: put the soft butter in a large mixing bowl, then mix using an electric beater while gradually adding the powdered sugar. Begin at the lowest speed, then raise it up to the medium speed until no more sugar is visible in the mixture. Incorporate the cream, the food coloring, and vanilla extract, then beat vigorously until the texture is even.

The icing should be thick and spread easily.

With a rather long kitchen knife, cut the cake into a large triangle (the shape of the hat). Spread the icing over the cake, then sprinkle it with the sour straws and non-pareils, etc. Decorate it with the candies to your liking.

Notes

☺ This is the famous yogurt cake recipe, the perfect base for many decorative cakes.

☺ If the icing is too runny, whisk in 2 tablespoons of sugar. If, on the other hand, it's too solid and cracks when you try to spread it, add 1 tablespoon of water (or more, but add 1 spoonful after another) and mix.

Christmas Tree

SERVES 6 PEOPLE

Preparation Time: 15 minutes

Baking Time: 45 minutes

⅔ cup of butter + a bit for the pan

About 9 oz. of mixed red fruits (strawberries, raspberries, redcurrants . . .)

4 eggs

About 9 oz. of sheep's milk cheese

Slightly under 1½ cups of flour

¾ cup of sugar

2 packets of vanilla sugar

1 packet of yeast

Round candies or bonbons

For the icing:

10½ oz. of green sugar paste (recipe on pg. 14) or almond paste (recipe on pg. 92)

Powdered sugar for spreading

Preheat the oven to 400°F.

Melt the butter. Wash the fruits and remove the stems. Cut the largest ones into 2 or 3 pieces. Separate the egg whites from the yolks. Using a food processor, chop up the sheep's milk cheese for 2 minutes. Add the egg yolks, one by one, then the melted butter. Blend. Pour in the sugar, the flour, and yeast. Whisk together vigorously until the batter is even.

Beat the egg whites until stiff. Add a third of the whites to the previous concoction, mixing these in gently, then add another third, mixing even more gently in order to not "break" these. Do the same for the rest of the whites.

Pour the batter into an already buttered springform pan shaped like a Christmas tree and bake for 15 minutes. Lower the oven to 350°F. Spread the red fruits on top and then continue baking for around 30 minutes. Let it cool before removing from the pan.

Spread the sugar paste or almond paste on a countertop, using a rolling pin (consider sprinkling the countertop and rolling pin with a little powdered sugar to keep the paste from sticking). Cover the Christmas tree in the sugar or almond paste and cut the excess away with a sharp knife. Decorate with round candies or bonbons.

Notes

☺   You can use frozen fruits, but avoid strawberries as these retain too much water.
Add the fruits to the batter while still frozen.

☺   If you do not have a Christmas tree-shaped pan, cut a round cake into the desired shape with a large knife.

Banzai Marble Cake

SERVES 8 PEOPLE

Preparation Time: 40 minutes

Baking Time: 40 minutes

3 eggs

1 cup of yogurt

2 cups of sugar

1 packet of vanilla sugar

1 cup of powdered sugar

1 pinch of salt

3 cups of flour

½ packet of baking powder

½ cup of oil

2 tbsps. of Nutella

Some sugar paste triangles
for decoration

Preheat the oven to 350°F.

Crack the eggs into a mixing bowl. Add the yogurt, stir, then pour in the sugars and salt. Stir vigorously. Add the flour and baking powder, beat, then pour in the oil. Mix gently at first, then more swiftly.

Split the batter in 2. Add the Nutella into one of the halves and mix well. Pour both halves of the batter, alternating between the plain batter and the Nutella batter, into an 8" springform pan. Bake for about 35 minutes. Check the doneness using the tip of a knife. The cake is finished when the tip emerges dry from the cake. Remove the cake from the oven, let it cool down, and then place it on a cooling rack.

Cut out a circle the size of the pan from a piece of paper. Place your hand in the middle and, using a pencil, trace the outline. In the middle of the outline, draw a smaller hand (about 4" long). Cut out this shape to make a stencil. When the cake has cooled, place your stencil onto it. Sprinkle with powdered sugar, then delicately remove your stencil. Repeat this process, placing the stencil back down to make a second hand. Finish decorating with the sugar paste triangles.

Notes

☺ Feel free to change the design on the cake by adding other ingredients (chocolate, icing, etc.) and decorating it with different shapes made of sugar paste.

Snowman

⅓ cup of butter + a bit for the pan

7 oz. of baking chocolate

2 tbsps. of flour

4 eggs

½ cup of sugar

A pinch of salt

3 Pocky biscuit sticks

1 ½ cups of powdered sugar

A little red almond paste for the hat (optional)

Tube of chocolate spread

Preheat the oven to 300°F.

Cut the butter into pieces. Break the chocolate into pieces and melt these in a double boiler or in the microwave (on low, stirring often). As soon as it has almost melted, add the butter, then the flour, and gently stir.

Separate the egg whites from the yolks. With an electric mixer, beat the yolks with the sugar, then add the melted chocolate and butter. Beat again. Using the electric mixer, now beat the egg whites with the salt until stiff. Add a third of the whites to the chocolate mix and beat. Using a spatula, mix the rest of the whites delicately until you have an even paste.

Butter a snowman-shaped springform pan (or 2 round springform pans, one 5 ½" across and the other 8 ½") Lay a piece of parchment paper on the bottom and pour in the mixture. Bake for 15 to 20 minutes.

During this time, cut the chocolate part of a Pocky into little pieces (to make the buttons and eyes). If you have some red almond paste, make a little knit hat.

Take out the cake and let it cool. If you are using 2 pans, take a cookie cutter and cut out a small circle from the top of the larger cake, which will become the body in order to have the smaller circle become the head. This will allow the smaller circle to fit together snugly with the larger circle and create the outline of the snowman. Place the large cake onto a rectangular plate and the small one in the corresponding hollow space.

Dust the snowman generously with powdered sugar. Stick 2 Pocky into the sides to make the arms. Place 2 little pieces of the Pocky as buttons, then 2 for the eyes. Stick the part of the Pocky without chocolate into the snowman as a nose (optional). Using a tube of chocolate spread, draw the mouth.

"Hello There!" Cake

**FOR 4 TO 6 PEOPLE
(USING A 10 ½ PAN)**

Preparation Time: 30 minutes

Baking Time: 40 minutes

⅓ cup of soft butter + a little for
the baking pan

2 packets of vanilla sugar or ½
of a very plump vanilla bean

1 cup of extra-fine powdered
sugar + a bit for the pan

¾ cup of flour

3 large egg whites

1¾ oz. of sugar cookie dough
(See recipe for Iced Sugar
Cookies on pg. 18)

1¾ oz. of dark or milk chocolate

Melt the butter, then let it cool completely. Add the vanilla sugar or if using the vanilla bean, split it in 2 lengthwise and scrape out the seeds. Set aside. Butter the bottom and the sides of a 10 ½" round pan, then sprinkle these with sugar. Place a circle of parchment paper on the bottom of the pan and chill it.

Preheat the oven to 325°F. Beat the egg whites until stiff using an electric beater. Once firm, add the powdered sugar. Beat until the meringue becomes very smooth and shiny. Then add the flour, pour in the vanilla butter, and gently stir with a flexible silicone spatula to avoid "breaking" the meringue. Keep stirring until the batter is quite smooth.

Pour the batter into the pan. Bake for about 30 to 40 minutes, until the top is good and golden. If the cake gets too golden, cover it with parchment paper.

While it's baking, draw a hand, about 2" tall, on a piece of paper. Cut it out. Roll out the cookie dough. Place the hand stencil onto the dough and use it to cut out 2 hands (one right and one left!) with a very sharp knife. Put these on a baking sheet covered in parchment paper and let bake for 10 minutes. Remove from the oven and allow to cool. Check whether the cake is done. Poke the tip of a knife into the cake; it should come back out clean. Delicately run the tip of a knife between the pan and the cake, then gently take out the cake. Remove the parchment paper and let the cake cool on a rack.

Melt the chocolate in a double boiler or microwave. With a paintbrush, coat each hand in chocolate. Unroll a piece of parchment paper, delicately pour a little chocolate onto it in the shape of a mouth and 2 eyes. Let chill and harden. When ready to serve, place the eyes, mouth, and hands onto the cake to create the desired emoticon. If needed, you can set the pieces in place with a little melted chocolate.

Cheesecake Heart

SERVES 8 PEOPLE

Preparation Time: 30 minutes

Baking Time: 1 hour
and 5 minutes

Let sit before serving: 3 hours

⅓ cup of butter + a bit
for the pan

7 oz. of shortbread cookies

3 eggs + 1 yolk

23 oz. of cream cheese (e.g.
Philadelphia, St Môret)

1 organic (or untreated) lemon

1 ½ cups of powdered sugar

1 tbsp. of flour

1½ tsps. of vanilla extract

For the sauce:

About 9 oz. of frozen red fruits

1 tbsp. of lemon juice

Slightly over ⅓ cup of
powdered sugar

Butter a heart-shaped springform pan with a removable bottom. Chop the cookies into fine crumbs in a bowl using a food processor. Add the butter and mix. Pour into the pan. Pack it down well using the bottom of a glass and let it chill.

Preheat the oven to 500°F.

In a bowl, beat the eggs together with the yolk. In a large mixing bowl, press the cream cheese with a fork to soften it. Wash and dry the lemon, then zest it over the cream cheese. Add the sugar, flour, and vanilla. Mix well. Add the eggs. Stir. Pour this cream into the pan. Bake for 5 minutes. Lower the oven to 210°F. Let it bake for 1 hour. Turn off the oven, open it gently and allow the cheesecake cool there. Once cool, place it in the refrigerator for at least 3 hours.

Prepare the sauce. While the cheesecake is baking, thaw the red fruits, drain them, and set aside the remaining juice. Squeeze the lemon. Mix the red fruits with the sugar and lemon juice. If the sauce seems too thick, add some spoonfuls of the fruits' juice. For a very smooth sauce, pour it through a chinois strainer to separate out the fruit pieces.

Remove the cheesecake from the refrigerator once it has gotten cold and firm, then spread the sauce delicately on top.

Notes

☺ Save the unused egg whites to make a royal icing (see pg. 18).
☺ The whites will keep very well if chilled in a bowl covered with a sheet of plastic.

Ghost Cake (lactose-free!)

Vegetable margarine
for the baking pan

½ cup of dark
chocolate (grated)

½ cup of coconut milk

Slightly over ½ cup of flour

1 oz. of bitter cocoa

1 heaping tsp. of baking powder

2 eggs

Slightly over ⅓ cup
of cane sugar

1 heaping tsp. of baking powder

1 pinch of salt

For the cream:

½ cup of vegetable margarine

½ tsp. of vanilla extract

1 ½ cups of powdered sugar

To decorate:

Black and pink sugar paste
(Recipe p. 14)

Preheat the oven to 350°F.

Coat an 8" rectangular pan with margarine and place a sheet of parchment paper at the bottom. Melt the grated dark chocolate into the coconut milk, either using a double boiler or a microwave (on low, stirring often). Sift together the flour, cocoa, and baking powder. Separate the egg whites from the yolks. Using an electric beater, vigorously beat the yolks and sugar. Gradually pour in the melted chocolate and stir well. Add in the flour-baking powder-cocoa blend. Mix.

Beat the egg whites with the salt until stiff, then incorporate these delicately into the batter. Pour into the pan and cook in the oven for 30 minutes.

Prepare the cream. Using an electric beater, beat together the margarine, vanilla, and half the sugar. Add the rest of the sugar and beat the cream until light and fluffy. Chill. Remove the cake from the oven, let it cool 15 minutes in the pan, then remove it from the pan.

Print or draw a ghost emoticon, about 8" tall. From this piece of paper, cut out the body and arms separately and lay them on the cake. Using a very sharp knife, cut out the body's outline on the cake. Do the same for the arms. Spread a little cream on the flat end of each arm and stick these to the ghost's body. Cover the ghost entirely with cream (the top and sides, too), smoothing it well with a spatula.

Roll out the black and pink sugar pastes. From the black paste, cut out a half-moon for the mouth and 2 circles (different sizes) for the eyes. Cut a tongue out from the pink paste. Use the dull side of the knife to draw a line in the middle of the tongue.

Notes

☺ **This lactose-free recipe is good for people who are lactose-intolerant or who just want to try something different . . . but you can also make it with a classic sponge cake and buttercream.**

Broken Heart Cake

1 cup of flour

1 tsp. baking powder

2 tsps. matcha tea powder

Slightly under ½ cup of butter + a little for the baking pan

2 eggs

¾ cup of powdered sugar + a little for the countertop

Slightly over ½ cup of ground almonds

1 pinch of salt

Red food coloring

9½ oz. of sugar paste or almond paste

Preheat the oven to 350°F.

Sift the flour, baking powder, and matcha tea in a mixing bowl. Melt the butter. Separate the egg whites from the yolks. Using an electric beater, beat the yolks together with the sugar and ground almonds. Pour in the melted butter and mix well, then add it all to the flour-baking powder-matcha tea mix and beat vigorously. Beat the egg whites with the salt until stiff. Using a spatula, mix them in delicately, in 3 separate pours.

Butter a heart-shaped baking pan. Lay a sheet of parchment paper on the bottom, pour in the batter and bake for about 35 minutes. Check if it's done (the knife tip should come back out dry). Let it cool before removing from the pan.

Add some drops of food coloring to the sugar paste (or almond paste), then roll it out, ensuring that you put a little powdered sugar to the countertop and the rolling pin to avoid it sticking.

Lay the paste delicately onto the cake and press it down so it sticks. Cut away the excess. Break the heart by cutting a zigzag from top to bottom and gently separate both halves.

Notes

☺ **Don't hesitate to prepare the sugar paste or almond paste yourself. (Recipes on p. 14 and 92)**
☺ **You can use the remaining paste to add all the visual details that you'd like.**

PANCAKES, WAFFLES, MOUSSES, ETC.

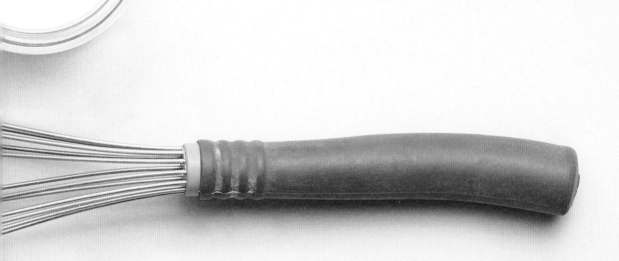

Waffles

MAKES ONE DOZEN WAFFLES

Preparation Time: 20 minutes

Let sit before serving: 30 minutes

Cooking Time: Around 4 minutes per waffle

¼ cup of butter

2 eggs

½ cup of sugar

1 packet of vanilla sugar

1 pinch of salt

1½ cups of milk

⅔ cup of half-and-half

3 heaping cups of flour

1 packet of baking powder

To decorate:

½ banana

Slightly over ¼ cup of chocolate

3 nice strawberries or raspberries

6 blueberries

Print emoticons the same size as your waffle maker (if it's not round, you can use a cookie cutter to shape the waffles once they are cooked).

Notes

 Use all types of fruit and let your imagination run wild. You can also use chocolate spread or food paste to decorate the waffles or crêpes!

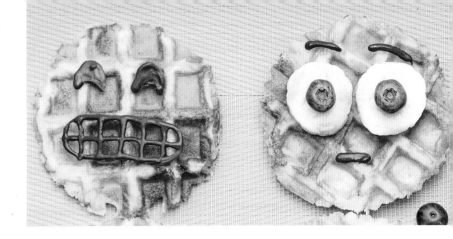

Prepare the waffle batter: melt the butter. Crack the eggs into a mixing bowl, add the sugar, vanilla sugar, and salt. Beat using an electric mixer. Pour in the milk and cream. Beat again. Add the flour and baking powder, whisk these together well, then pour in the butter and mix one last time. Let the batter rest for at least 30 minutes.

Lay your printed emoticons on a piece of parchment paper. Melt the chocolate in a double boiler or microwave (on medium, stirring regularly).

Fill a piping bag with a rather fine nozzle and trace the emoticons' patterns to draw the eyes and different mouth shapes. Let it harden. Meanwhile, cut the banana into rounds, cut the strawberries into slices, and carve hearts inside them.

Heat the waffle maker. Once hot, put a little batter in the middle of the waffle maker. Waffles are cooked when golden. Put the waffles onto a plate, then adorn with the decorations you have prepared: the chocolate eyes and mouths, as well as the strawberry or raspberry hearts for eyes or to make a kissing mouth, or blueberries on top of the banana rounds to form eyes.

Mini Love Pancakes

SERVES 6 PEOPLE

Preparation Time: 10 minutes

Refrigerate: 2 hours

Cook time: 15 minutes

2 eggs

Slightly under ⅔ cup of sugar

1 packet of vanilla sugar

2 cups of milk

½ cup of neutral oil
(e.g. sunflower oil) + a little
bit for the skillet

Slightly under 2 cups of flour

1 packet of yeast

1 pinch of salt

Some pink candy hearts

1 tube of chocolate spread

Beat the eggs, sugar, and vanilla sugar in a mixing bowl using an electric beater. Add the milk, then the oil. In another mixing bowl, mix the flour, yeast, and salt, then add these into the previous mixture via separate pours, stirring well after each pour. Whisk together until the batter is even. Cover, then chill for at least 2 hours.

Prepare the mini pancakes. Heat a little oil in a pan over rather high heat. When the pan is good and hot, pour in 1 spoonful of batter, lower the heat, and let it cook 2 to 3 minutes on each side on medium heat. Repeat the process until you have used all the batter.

Dampen the candy hearts lightly. Place these onto each pancake where the eyes would be and draw a mouth with the chocolate.

Notes

☺   You can cut little hearts from strawberries, red apples, almond paste, or anything else you desire.
☺   For identically shaped pancakes, you can cut them again with a round cookie cutter or a glass.

"Hurts So Good" Chocolate Mousse

SERVES 6 PEOPLE

Preparation Time: 15 minutes

Cooking Time: 10 minutes

Let sit before serving: 6 hours

Slightly under ¼ cup of butter

¾ cup of dark chocolate chips

¾ cup of white chocolate chips

4 heaping tbsps. of powdered sugar

6 eggs

Split the butter in 2 and cut it into small pieces. Put ¾ cup of dark chocolate in a bowl and ¾ cup of white chocolate in another bowl. Melt them in the microwave (on low, stirring often) or in a double boiler (place a mixing bowl onto a saucepan filled a third of the way with hot water—the bottom of the mixing bowl should not touch the water—and let it melt, on medium heat, while stirring). When the chocolates have both nearly melted, add to each bowl one half of the butter pieces. Continue to melt the mixture while stirring.

Take 3 eggs and separate the whites from the yolks. Using an electric beater, beat the yolks together with 3 tablespoons of sugar. Add the dark chocolate and beat vigorously. Beat the egg whites until stiff. Add a third of the white chocolate to the dark chocolate and mix vigorously. Using a spatula, delicately incorporate the remaining whites by adding one half first, then the other to avoid "breaking the balance." Pour this mousse into 3 small bowls or glasses.

Repeat these same steps for the white chocolate, but do not add more than 1 tablespoon of sugar. Cover and place the 6 ramekins to chill for at least 6 hours.

Remove the mousse from the refrigerator and decorate. Separately melt the remaining white and dark chocolate and place these into 2 piping bags. Using a fine-tipped nozzle, delicately draw the bandage with the white chocolate. With the dark chocolate, draw the eyes and mouth.

Notes

☺ You can make a mini-slit at the very end of your piping bag to let out a thin strip of chocolate or you can use a "writing" nozzle (fine-tipped) to draw with greater precision.

Rice Pudding

FOR 6 TO 8 PEOPLE

Preparation Time: 10 minutes

Cooking Time: 1 hour 20

1 vanilla bean

4¼ cups of milk

⅔ cup of round rice (special dessert rice or round Camargue rice, for example)

½ cup of sugar

1 licorice coil

Split the vanilla bean lengthwise into 2 pieces using the tip of a knife. Place into a saucepan along with the milk. Raise the temperature to boiling, remove from the stovetop and let it steep. In a saucepan, cover most of the rice with water. Bring to a boil, lower the heat and simmer for 15 minutes.

Preheat the oven to 350°F.

Drain the rice, then pour into a baking dish. Remove the vanilla bean from the milk, then pour the milk onto the rice. Add the sugar and stir. Cook for about 1 hour. During this hour, stir it 3 times.

Remove the rice from the oven and serve into small glasses or ramekins (between 6 to 8 containers, depending on their size). Let cool.

Prepare the decorations. Uncoil the licorice. Split the double coil to create a finer strip. Cut into the size needed to make eyes and mouths. Try also to keep the middle of the licorice coiled up, to form one of the mouths. Decorate the rice pudding with the licorice pieces.

Notes

☺ You can make the recipe family-style by leaving the rice in the baking dish.

☺ Be sure to mix it before chilling, as a thin crust will form on top. While certainly tasty, this will not be pretty under your decorations.

☺ For even more vanilla flavor, after steeping it, remove the vanilla bean and scrape the seeds into the milk using the dull edge of the knife. If you don't have a vanilla bean, add vanilla sugar while lowering the rest of the sugar amounts in the recipe, or use a little cinnamon powder (about ½ tsp.) instead.

☺ You could also make the decorations from chocolate (see the decorations used in the waffle recipe on p. 64).

Angry Panna Cotta

SERVES 4 PEOPLE

Preparation Time: 20 minutes

Cooking Time: 15 minutes

Refrigerate: 2 hours

2 gelatin leaves

1 vanilla bean

3 cups of heavy whipping cream (*substitute: 3 ½ cups of yogurt)

½ cup of caster sugar

For the sauce:

4 cups of frozen red fruits

⅓ cup of sugar (or ½ cup, if you prefer it sweeter)

To decorate:

White chocolate spread or slightly over ¼ cup of white chocolate

Soak the gelatin leaves in a bowl of cold water. Cut the vanilla bean in 2 lengthwise and add it to the cream in a saucepan. Bring to a boil and let it boil for 5 minutes while stirring frequently, the add the caster sugar and stir until you have an even cream. Remove from the stovetop. Take out the vanilla bean and scrape the seeds into the cream.

Squeeze the gelatin leaves dry by pressing them between your hands. Add these to the cream. Stir well to dissolve completely. Let rest about 1 minute and stir again. Pour the cream into 6 small containers (shot glasses, ramekins, cups, etc.). Cover these, allow to cool, then chill for at least 2 hours.

Prepare the sauce. Pour the fruit and sugar into a saucepan. Cover and bring to a boil on medium heat. Let it cook 5 minutes while covered, stirring from time to time, then remove the lid and cook another 2 minutes. Whisk gently with an electric mixer and let it cool.

Take the panna cottas out of the refrigerator. Pour red fruit sauce onto each panna cotta, then, with the chocolate spread, draw the eyes and mouth. If you've chosen to use chocolate chips, melt these, put them into a piping bag, and draw the emoticon.

Notes

☺ To check whether the panna cotta has "set," shake the container gently. If it has set, the cream should not quiver.

SAVORY RECIPES

Kissing Omelet

SERVES 6 PEOPLE

Preparation Time: 20 minutes

Cook Time: 45 minutes

½ lb. of potatoes

5 tbsps. of oil

1 clove of garlic

2 ⅘ oz. of chorizo + 2 pieces for decoration

2 tbsps. of parsley, finely chopped

6 eggs

Salt

1 knife tip's worth of chili pepper

Peel the potatoes, wash them, and cut into rounds ¼" to ½" thick. Peel the garlic clove and finely chop it. Cut the chorizo into thin strips.

Preheat the oven to 400°F.

Heat the oil in a large frying pan and lightly brown the potatoes, stirring often. Add the garlic, chorizo, and parsley. Mix and cook another 3 minutes, minding that the garlic does not burn. Remove from the heat and flip it all onto a plate.

Whisk the eggs with a little salt and chili pepper, then add the potatoes and chorizo. Flip the blend into a springform pan (about 2" tall). Cook in the oven for about 25 minutes, until the omelet has set.

During this time, cut the chorizo into whatever shapes you like: a kissy-mouth, eyes, eyebrows, or a heart, depending on what you want! Remove the omelet from the oven and decorate it.

Notes

☺ You can use precooked potatoes, but consider sautéing these; that will really give them flavor.
☺ When decorating, let your imagination and seasonal crops inspire. Vegetables and their colors can spark a wealth of ideas.

Mini Pizzas

FOR 4 TO 6 PEOPLE

Preparation Time: 30 minutes

Cooking Time: 10 + 10 minutes

3 ½ oz. of aged Parmesan

Some sprigs of fresh rosemary

7 oz. of frozen pizza crust (preferably in ball form) or fresh dough from the bakery

Flour for the countertop

Some fine slices of capocollo/ coppa or salami or 3 slices of raw ham

Extra virgin olive oil

To decorate:

Some button mushrooms

Some pitted black olives

Preheat the oven to 400°F.

Grate the Parmesan using the large holes on a cheese grater or chop it into fine slices. Coarsely chop the rosemary. Cut the dough in 2 before rolling it out (about ⅛" thick) on the kitchen counter lightly covered in flour, using a rolling pin. With a cookie cutter or a glass, form circles from the dough. Put these one by one onto a plate covered with parchment paper.

With the same cookie cutter, cut circles in the middle of the slices of coppa, salami, or ham (if you use a glass, cut the ham all along the rim of the glass with a very sharp knife). Clean the mushrooms and use the knife to cut out some mouths from these. Cut some olive slices to make the eyes.

Sprinkle a little fresh rosemary and Parmesan on the dough circles and add a dash of olive oil. Add the coppa/ salami/ham rounds, decorate with olive eyes and mushroom mouths. Cook in the oven for about 10 minutes. During this time, prepare the second batch with the remaining dough and ingredients.

Remove the mini pizzas from the oven and serve hot.

Notes

☺ These pizzas are better hot. Put the second tray into the oven as soon as the first pizzas are done.
☺ You can also spread a little tomato sauce onto the dough and add cheese.
☺ To speed up the decoration, add olive pieces for eyes, whole rosemary sprigs for the mouth, and little pieces of pepper, onion, and mushroom.

Stunned Zucchini Tart

SERVES 4 TO 6 PEOPLE

Preparation Time: 20 minutes

Cooking Time: 50 minutes

2 firm zucchinis

1 clove of garlic

4 tbsps. of oil olive

4 eggs

2 tbsps. of cottage cheese

2 tbsps. of flour

2 tbsps. of grated Parmesan

2 tbsps. of mint, finely chopped

1 pitted black olive

Wash and dry the zucchinis. Cut off the ends. Slice 2 rather fine rounds from the zucchini as well as a piece about 1 ½" long. Grate the rest using the large holes on a cheese grater.

Peel the garlic clove and cut it into thirds.

Heat 2 tablespoons of olive oil in a nonstick pan. Add the garlic, let it brown for 1 minute before adding the shredded zucchini. Let it get golden-brown for 5 minutes, then remove the garlic and the pan from the stovetop.

Crack the eggs in a mixing bowl, beat them, then add the zucchini, cottage cheese, flour, parmesan, and mint. Mix. Pour the egg mixture into the pan along with the remaining oil. Cook for 20 minutes on medium heat, then 5 minutes in the oven broiler.

Flip the tart onto a large plate. Place the 2 fine zucchini rounds on the tart like eyes. Cut 2 slices of olive and place these in the middle of the "zucchini eyes." Cut the eyebrows and mouth from the remaining zucchini slice.

Notes

☺ You can make a blend of carrots and zucchinis. In that case, put the carrots into the pan 1 minute before the zucchinis. For a complete dish, you can add cubes of cooked ham or little pieces of chicken.

Potato, Bacon, and Cheddar Quiche

FOR 4 TO 6 PEOPLE

Preparation Time: 30 minutes

Cooking Time: 1 hour

Let sit before serving: 30 minutes

⅔ lb. of potatoes

2 pre-made puff pastry crusts

4 eggs

1 onion

⅓ lb. of bacon

5 ½ oz. of cheddar

⅘ cup of light whipping cream

3 tbsps. of oil (olive or another)

1 tbsp. of curry or thyme (optional)

Salt and freshly ground pepper

Notes

☺ Opt always for puff pastry crust made with pure butter.

☺ There really is a difference in quality . . . look at the ingredients.

☺ You can make the same tart with piecrust. There's no use in pre-baking the crust, but do let it bake at least 35 minutes.

☺ For the small emoticons, there's no sense in baking them on 2 sheets/trays.

Set the potatoes to cook in salt water. Drain and peel.

Preheat the oven to 400°F. Roll out a puff pastry crust. Using a cookie cutter (or a glass) cut out some circles at whatever size you like. With a small tube or straw, cut out some eyes and, with the tip of a very sharp knife, a mouth.

Whisk 1 egg, add a pinch of salt, and baste each little emoticon using a brush with the whisked egg. Lay the emoticons on a piece of parchment paper and place them on a baking tray. Cover them with another piece of parchment paper and a broiler rack. Cook for 15 to 20 minutes (the crust should be quite golden). Remove from the oven and allow to cool.

Peel and finely chop the onion. Cut the cheddar into pieces. Heat a pan on a hot stove. Add the bacon and brown for 3 minutes. Remove from the stove and set aside.

Add the onion and the thyme or curry into the pan, stir, cover, and let sauté for 5 minutes. Cut the potatoes into small pieces. Add to the onions, stir, and let cook for 5 minutes, adding oil if needed. Put in the bacon, stir once more, and remove from the fire.

Roll out the other dough and place it into a pie dish about 8" across. Cover with parchment paper and pie weights. Lower the oven temperature to 350°F and bake the tart for 10 minutes. Delicately remove the parchment paper and put the tart back into the oven for 5 minutes. Take the dish from the oven and spread the mixture of bacon, potatoes, and onions onto the crust. Add the cheddar. Crack the remaining eggs in a mixing bowl. Whisk them, add the cream, season with salt and pepper, then gently pour the mixture onto the tart. Bake for 20 minutes. Remove from the oven and decorate with the little emojis. Serve right away.

Mini Thumbs Up Grilled Ham-and-Cheese Sandwich

MAKES 8 SANDWICHES

Preparation Time: 30 minutes

Cooking Time: About
10 minutes

8 slices of white bread

A food decorating pen

6 generous slices of
cooked ham

Slightly over 1 cup of
heavy cream

2 cups of grated cheese
(Emmental or Beaufort)

Slightly under ¼ cup of butter

Freshly ground pepper

Cut the bread slices into fourths, to make 8 squares. On a piece of paper, draw, using a food decorating pen, a hand with a thumbs up, the same size as the bread slice. Lay the drawing on top of a slice of bread and cut around this outline. Repeat these steps for the other slices and do the same for the pieces of ham, setting aside the off cuts.

Preheat the oven to 400°F.

Mix the cream and cheese, then pepper them. Spread this cream mixture onto the slices of white bread. Add the slices of ham as well as the off cuts, if needed. Finish off the ham-and-cheese sandwich with a second slice of white bread (after spreading the cream on the inside). Melt the butter and generously spread it over the slices of bread. Put it in the oven until golden brown.

Notes

☺ You can add some zucchini slices, fried golden brown in a skillet with olive oil.

Semolina Tartlets

SERVES 6 PEOPLE

Preparation Time: 30 minutes

Cooking Time: 50 minutes

Let sit before serving:
15 minutes

⅓ cup of butter + a bit for browning

4 ¼ cups of milk

A little ground nutmeg

Salt

1 heaping cup of medium-grade semolina

1 egg (beaten)

1 cup of grated Parmesan

To decorate:

Ketchup

Cut the butter into little pieces. Pour the milk into a saucepan, then add the butter and ground nutmeg, and salt it. Bring to a boil, then sprinkle in the semolina and beat swiftly for about 5 minutes. As soon as the semolina is cooked and its consistency is rather dense, take it off the burner. Add the beaten egg and slightly under 1 cup of grated Parmesan. Mix well.

Spread on a plate (or onto a baking pan covered with parchment paper) so it's just under ½ inch thick. Pat it down well and smooth with a spatula or the back of a large spoon. Let it cool down completely.

Preheat the oven to 400°F.

Cut the tartlets with a glass or a cookie cutter (whatever shape you like). Wet these with a little water and dip both sides into the rest of the grated Parmesan. Then place them, gently overlapping, in a large oven dish. Add some generous pats of butter and let it brown for 15 to 20 minutes.

Put the ketchup into a pastry/piping bag. Remove the little tarts from the oven and decorate them using piping tips. Serve with a green salad.

Notes

☺ If you don't have different cookie cutters, you can draw the shapes you want on a piece of parchment paper, cut these out, and lay them on the cold dough before cutting out the shapes with a very sharp knife. When making them, you can change the decorations and ingredients.

☺ Try using a tapenade instead of ketchup or adding little pieces of tomato/olive/zucchini on top of each little tart before putting them in the oven.

Small Bites + Gourmet Selection

Homemade Almond Paste

MAKES 7 OZ. OF ALMOND PASTE ☺ Preparation Time: 10 minutes ☺ Bake Time: 10 minutes

1 heaping cup of ground almonds • ¾ cup of powdered sugar + a bit more for decoration • 4 tsps. of water • 2 tsps. of orange blossom water, rose water, rum, or bitter almond extract

Preheat the oven to 300°F.

Spread the ground almonds onto a baking sheet. Put it in the oven and let them dry for 10 minutes.

Mix together the ground almonds and the sugar, then add the water and the orange blossom/rose water, alcohol, or bitter almond extract.

Knead the dough quickly in a mixing bowl until it becomes thick and even. Sprinkle with powdered sugar and wrap in plastic. It will keep for up to a week in the refrigerator.

Bread Pudding

SERVES 4 PEOPLE ☺ Preparation Time: 10 minutes ☺ Bake Time: 10 minutes

1 vanilla bean • ½ cup of milk • 2 eggs • ⅓ cup of sugar • 8 slices of day-old brioche • Just under ¼ cup of butter

Split the vanilla bean in 2, scrape out the seeds and put them into the milk. Whisk the eggs with the sugar, then add the vanilla milk.

Using the tip of a knife, cut out eyes and mouths from the brioche. Dunk both sides of the brioche slices in the milk-egg-sugar mix and let soak.

Melt the butter in a frying pan, then add the slices of brioche. Let them turn golden-brown on medium heat, for about 3 minutes on each side. Serve with red fruits and fresh cream.

Chocolate Sauce

SERVES 4 PEOPLE ☺ Preparation Time: 5 minutes ☺ Cooking Time: 15 minutes

⅓ cup of dark chocolate • 2 oz. of light whipping cream • 1 heaping tablespoonful of powdered sugar

Grind the chocolate into a fine powder. Bring the chocolate, cream, and sugar to a boil in a small saucepan with 3½ ounces of water.

Stir until the chocolate melts and the sugar dissolves. Lower the heat and continue mixing until the cream becomes thick and smooth (it should coat the spoon like a crème anglaise).

Serve right away or cover immediately, let it cool, and refrigerate it.

Smiley Face Mini-Potato Tarts

SERVES 4 PEOPLE ☺ Preparation Time: 20 minutes ☺ Cooking Time: 40 minutes

3 large potatoes • 3 tbsps. corn starch • 1 tbsp. flour + a little for cooking • 3 tbsps. of bread crumbs • Salt, pepper • 1 egg (beaten) • 1 dash of oil

Rinse the large potatoes in clean water. Peel them and cut them first into quarters, then into pieces. Cook them in boiling salt water for 15 to 20 minutes (they should be quite soft). Drain them, then pour them onto a large platter. Add the cornstarch, flour, and breadcrumbs. Salt, pepper, and then mash using a fork. Add the beaten egg and stir it in well.

Place the parchment paper on a flat surface and sprinkle it with flour. Spread the potatoes on it and sprinkle more flour. Cover with baking paper and flatten with a rolling pin. Remove the paper and, using a round cookie cutter (or a glass or a cup), makes circles on the potato dough.

Draw the eyes with a straw and the mouth with a spoon.

Put the oil in a frying pan and fry the mini-cakes in the hot oil for 20 minutes.

Useful Measurements

1 PAD OF BUTTER =
0.15 oz.

1 CHUNK OF BUTTER = 0.52 oz.

1 TEASPOON (TSP.) =
→ 0.17 oz. of Salt, Sugar, or Oil
→ 0.25 oz. of butter
→ 0.17 oz. of liquid
→ 0.17 oz. of flour or semolina

1 TABLESPOON (TBSP.)
→ 0.50 oz. of sugar, flour, or butter
→ 0.4 oz. of crème fraîche or oil
→ 0.50 oz. of liquid
→ 3 teaspoons

1 PINCH OF SALT =
0.01–0.02 oz.

1 CUBE OF SUGAR =
0.17 oz.

Oven Temperatures

THERMOSTAT	APPROXIMATE TEMPERATURE
1	**86°F** (Barely lukewarm)
2	**140°F** (Lukewarm)
3	**194°F** (Very slightly hot)
4	**248°F** (Slightly hot)
5	**302°F** (Moderately hot)
6	**356°F** (Medium heat)
7	**410°F** (Rather hot)
8	**464°F** (Hot)
9	**518°F** (Very hot)
10	**572°F** (High heat)

Index

Angry Panna Cotta, *74*

Apple of My Eye Cake, *40*

Banzai Marble Cake, *50*

Bread Pudding, *92*

Broken Heart Cake, *60*

Cake Pops, *26*

Cheesecake Heart, *56*

Chocolate Sauce, *93*

Chocolate Side Eye Cookies, *24*

Christmas Tree, *48*

Cloud Shortbreads, *22*

Feet Cookies, *20*

French Ice Cream Macarons, *34*

Ghost Cake (lactose-free!), *58*

Gift Cake, *42*

"Hello There!" Cake, *54*

Homemade Almond Paste, *92*

Homemade Sugar Paste, *14*

"Hurts So Good" Chocolate Mousse, *70*

Iced Emoji Sugar Cookies, *18*

Kiss Omelet, *78*

Mini Love Pancakes, *68*

Mini Pizzas, *80*

Mini Thumbs Up Ham-and-Cheese Sandwich, *88*

Party Hat, *46*

Pig Biscuits, *30*

Poop Cupcakes, *32*

Poop Meringues, *36*

Potato, Bacon, Cheddar Quiche, *84*

Semolina Tartlets, *90*

Smiley Face Mini Potato Tarts, *92*

Snowman, *52*

Stunned Zucchini Tart, *82*

Rice Pudding, *72*

Waffles, *64*

Skyhorse Publishing books may be purchased in bulk at special discounts for sales promotion, corporate gifts, fund-raising, or educational purposes.Special editions can also be created to specifications. For details, contact the Special Sales Department, Skyhorse Publishing, 307 West 36th Street, 11th Floor, New York, NY 10018 or info@skyhorsepublishing.com.

Skyhorse® and Skyhorse Publishing® are registered trademarks of Skyhorse Publishing, Inc.®, a Delaware corporation.

Visit our website at www.skyhorsepublishing.com.

10 9 8 7 6 5 4 3 2 1

Library of Congress Cataloging-in-Publication Data is available on file.

Print ISBN: 978-1-5107-3412-8
E-Book ISBN: 978-1-5107-3413-5

Editor in Chief: Didier Férat
Editing: Marjorie Goussu
Graphics: Julia Philipps

Layout and Photoengraving: APS-Chromostyle Fabrication: Laurence Duboscq

Printed in China